TRADE AND
GLOBAL IMPACT

BY SHEELAGH MATTHEWS

Weigl

Published by Weigl Educational Publishers Limited
6325 10th Street SE
Calgary, Alberta
T2H 2Z9

Website: www.weigl.com

Library and Archives Canada Cataloguing in Publication data available upon request.
Fax (403) 233-7769 for the attention of the Publishing Records department.

ISBN 978-1-55388-693-8 (hard cover)
ISBN 978-1-55388-698-3 (soft cover)

Printed in the United States of America in North Mankato, Minnesota
1 2 3 4 5 6 7 8 9 0 14 13 12 11 10

072010
WEP230610

All of the Internet URLs given in the book were valid at the time of publication. However, due to the
dynamic nature of the Internet, some addresses may have changed, or sites may have ceased to exist
since publication. While the author and publisher regret any inconvenience this may cause readers, no
responsibility for any such changes can be accepted by either the author or the publisher.

Weigl acknowledges Getty Images as its primary image supplier for this title.

Every reasonable effort has been made to trace ownership and to obtain permission to reprint copyright
material. The publishers would be pleased to have any errors or omissions brought to their attention so
that they may be corrected in subsequent printings.

We acknowledge the financial support of the Government of Canada through the Canada Book Fund
for our publishing activities.

EDITOR: Josh Skapin
DESIGN: Terry Paulhus

Trade and Global Impact
Contents

Trade and Global Impact
Through The Years

Trading is the way the world exchanges goods. It has allowed people to exchange one kind of good for another of equal value. Ideally, trade happens in a fair and equitable manner.

In the 1600s and 1700s, Canada's prosperity came from its raw natural resources and the value placed on selling these resources to other countries. Such resources are called **exports**. Great Britain's interest in furs and timber brought early wealth to Canada. Later, in the 19th and 20th centuries, Canada made money by mining and trading its raw mineral resources, such as coal, nickel, copper, gold and silver. Once Canada's cross-country transportation routes were established, trade started occurring between provinces. For example, agricultural products from the Prairies were exported to Ontario and Quebec.

Throughout most of the 20th century, Canada was known for more than just its natural resources. Processing and manufacturing raw materials to make cars, equipment, building components, foods, and other goods, including weapons to fight two world wars, created jobs for the growing Canadian population.

As the world's population expanded, there was an increased demand for Canadians to manufacture and ship goods and services of all kinds. This gave Canada's oil and gas resources greater value in the global marketplace. Today, Canada's wealth is mainly associated with its energy, agricultural, and water resources. This has resulted in the Canadian **economy** being based on a **petro dollar** in the late 20th and early 21st centuries.

Canada's economy is fuelled by more than the non-renewable sources of oil and gas, however. Canada also has a well-educated population, a necessity for a nation to be competitive in the **Information Age**. As a result, innovation is a large part of the nation's output. Canadians across the country are discovering and developing green energy-saving technologies, producing information and communication technologies (ICT), and making important medical breakthroughs. All of the innovations are to share with the world through trade.

2000s

Free Trade Fast Track

GDP versus GPI

2000s

Free Trade Fast Track

The 2000s saw Canada renegotiating **free trade** agreements (FTAs) all around the world. Several types of free trade arrangements were being revised, including the 1994 Agreement on Internal Trade (AIT), for interprovincial trade. This agreement was amended in 2009 to further eliminate trade barriers and enhance **labour mobility** between all the provinces. As a result, people working in professions that are licensed provincially, such as physicians, can work in different provinces without acquiring a new license for each province. The North American Free Trade Agreement (NAFTA) remained in place throughout the 2000s. NAFTA is an agreement signed by Canada, Mexico, and the United States that reduces or eliminates trade barriers, such as tariffs, between the three nations. In an effort to break down even more trade barriers, Canada, the United States, and Mexico were involved in talks concerning a project called the Security and Prosperity Partnership (SPP). The SPP would ensure that public resources, such as energy, were easily accessible to private interests, such as corporations. The SPP made some people fear for Canada's ability to sustainably manage its resources of energy and water.

2000s

GDP versus GPI

Countries often measure their economic success in terms of **Gross Domestic Product (GDP)**. This refers to the amount of economic activity taking place in a nation. As long as a dollar value can be attached to an activity, it is included in the nation's GDP. In late 2009 and early 2010, Desjardins Group, the largest association of credit unions in North America, studied the economic growth of several countries around the world. According to the group's

2001

North America is affected by terrorist attacks on the World Trade Center in New York City.

2002

Mad Cow disease impacts Canada's beef industry.

2003

Canada opts out of joining the U.S.-led coalition to fight Iraq because the United Nations (UN) does not sanction the confrontation.

findings, Canada's overall GDP increased by more than three percent in 2010. Canada surpassed the U.S. growth rate of 2.7 percent, making Canada the fastest-growing economy of all the G7 nations. An alternative to the GDP is the Genuine Progress Indicator (GPI). This index measures the economic value of an activity and the social and environmental aspects.

Summit of the Americas

Summit of the Americas is a series of meetings between the leaders of North American, Central American, South American, and Caribbean nations. During the meetings, the leaders discuss a number of issues, including free trade. Quebec City hosted the 3rd Summit of the Americas from April 20 to 22, 2001. At the summit, a plan was approved to create the world's largest free trade zone by December 2005. The proposed free trade area would stretch from Alaska to Argentina. This would include about 15 percent of the world's population. By 2010, the Free Trade Area of the Americas Agreement (FTAA) was still a work in progress.

Summit of the Americas

2004

Air Canada no longer requires bankruptcy protection.

2005

For the first time in 30 years, Canada sends naval vessels to the Arctic to protect Canada's interest in the North.

British Columbia and Alberta Sign Agreement

In 2006, British Columbia Premier Gordon Campbell and Alberta Premier Ralph Klein signed the Trade, Investment and Labour Mobility Agreement (TILMA). TILMA allowed workers, such as teachers and plumbers, who are certified to work in one province to work in the other province as well. In addition, TILMA gave individuals and companies the right to sue the provincial government over any rules or regulations that they felt restricted their trade or investment. As such, the agreement favoured corporate interests over a local government authority. On July 1, 2010, TILMA was expanded to include Saskatchewan. The new agreement is known as the New West Partnership Trade Agreement (NWPTA) and incudes the same commitments and obligations as TILMA.

British Columbia and Alberta Sign Agreement - Ralph Klein

2006

Stephen Harper, leader of the Conservative Party, becomes prime minister of Canada.

2007

Media mogul Conrad Black is sentenced to prison and fined for misusing funds from his former newspaper empire.

Global Financial Crisis

Climate Change

2008

Global Financial Crisis

In 2008, the North American economy went from boom to bust. Referred to as the Global Financial Crisis (GFC), there was massive unemployment due to banks tightening up on giving loans to businesses. The United States bailed out large banks and corporations with a cash injection of $700 billion in an attempt to avoid a massive economic collapse across its nation. Canada did likewise with a $75 billion bank bailout. A bailout is when money is given to an organization to help it avoid bankruptcy. The Canadian bank bailout was made through the Canada Housing and Mortgage Corporation (CMHC). The CMHC is a provider of mortgage loan insurance and housing policies and programs. The Canadian government purchased $50 billion in insured **mortgage pools** from the CMHC, causing an increase of $75 billion.

2009

Climate Change

The connection between humankind and the environment was the topic of the 15th Conference of the Parties (COP15) during the 2009 United Nations Climate Change Conference, or Copenhagen Summit. Talks focussed on setting the highest possible targets for **carbon emissions** in the fight against climate change. Canada did not support the established targets because energy is one of its primary resources and the production of energy causes carbon emissions.

Into the Future

Climate change is an important issue for the nation and around the world. Think about issues that threaten climate change in Canada. How can you help make your home or community a greener place to live? What can Canadians do to help meet environmental standards established at conferences such as COP15?

2008	2009	2010
The U.S. goods **trade deficit** with Canada is $78.3 billion.	Canada does not support setting the highest targets for carbon emissions.	Canada signs a free trade agreement with Panama.

NAFTA

1992

NAFTA

In 1992, Canada, the United States, and Mexico finalized the terms of the North American Free Trade Agreement (NAFTA) to promote financial improvement for all three countries. Taking effect two years later, on January 1, 1994, NAFTA eliminated most barriers to trade, such as costly tariffs and taxes, between these three countries over the next 15 years. From a purely economic standpoint, NAFTA was considered a success, as total trade among the three countries more than doubled. However, Canada experienced many job losses due to NAFTA. Transnational corporations, companies that own or invest in production facilities in more than one country, benefitted greatly from NAFTA. They were able to take advantage of inexpensive resources and labour to produce goods in the most profitable way possible.

1991

Trade negotiations begin between Canada, the United States, and Mexico.

1992

Cod fishing on the Grand Banks is halted by the Canadian government to help protect over-fished cod stocks.

RCMP and Disney

1995

RCMP and Disney

For years, many companies produced and profited from low-quality merchandise that displayed the Mountie image. In 1995, the Royal Canadian Mounted Police took measures to ensure its image would no longer be misused. The RCMP gave the Walt Disney Company a five-year contract to handle the promotion and marketing of RCMP products. As a result, anyone wanting to use the Mountie image on T-shirts or dolls, for example, had to acquire permission and pay a fee for the right to do so. Failure to do so could result in theft charges. Many people had mixed feelings about the decision to hire an American company to protect a Canadian symbol.

However, the RCMP said it was important that they choose a partner that had experience and success in marketing. The contract with the Walt Disney Company expired in 1999, and the Mounties took back control of their own marketing. As of 2002, more than $1 million from the sales of Mountie mugs, plush bears, pens, and other items was donated to projects meant to enhance the safety of Canadians.

1993

Canada's merchandise trade with Europe is more than $32 billion.

1994

NAFTA comes into effect on January 1, 1994.

1995

The World Trade Organization begins operations on January 1, 1995.

Kyoto Protocol

The Kyoto Protocol was adopted by 160 nations at the 1997 United Nations conference on climate change in Kyoto, Japan. The protocol was an environmental treaty calling for reduction in the production of greenhouse gases. Included in the agreement was a target for 34 industrialized countries to reduce their greenhouse gas emissions by 5.2 percent below their levels in 1990. In 2005, the province of Alberta filed a formal objection to the federal government's plans to observe the Kyoto Protocol, claiming it would hurt the province's oil and gas industry. In 2007, under a government led by Prime Minister Stephen Harper, Canada stopped attempting to meet the Kyoto Protocol's greenhouse gas reduction targets.

Kyoto Protocol

1996

Craig Kielburger, a 13-year-old boy from Ontario, speaks out against child labour at Canada's trade mission in India.

1997

Drilling begins at Hibernia, an oil field off the coast of Newfoundland.

Y2K

Y2K

World trade and business transactions of any kind nearly came to a halt when the clock struck midnight at the turn of the century. People around the world feared that a possible computer error could cause computers systems around the world to stop working. When computers were first built, a computer code required only two digits to represent a year. For example, the number 96 would refer to the year 1996. When the clock struck midnight in the year 2000, four digits would be needed to indicate the year. Entering the number "00" would revert back to the year 1900. As most industries had become computerized, from banking and phone communication to the transmission of power and energy, companies and governments spent billions of dollars to find and fix the Y2K glitch in their computer codes. Due to all the effort ahead of time, everything worked just fine when the world entered the 21st century.

Into the Future

If computers had failed on New Year's Day in the year 2000, it would not have been possible for businesses to operate. Imagine the "glitch" in computer systems had not been corrected. What would have happened to trade relations across the globe? How would businesses function? What would your life be like without the use of computers?

1998	1999	2000
Canada is one of the first countries to sign the Kyoto Protocol.	Air Canada takes control of Canadian Airlines.	Organization of American States, meetings take place in Windsor, Canada.

National Energy Program

The Constitution Act

1980

National Energy Program

In 1980, Liberal Prime Minister Pierre Trudeau introduced the National Energy Program (NEP). The NEP was designed to protect Canadians from the shock of high global oil prices while helping the country become self-sufficient in energy. The program was a sustainable approach to Canadians' immediate and long-term energy needs. Among other things, the NEP forced Canadian oil companies to sell their oil below global market prices, costing the industry billions of dollars in profits. Many people living in Alberta, where much of Canada's oil is produced,

were upset with the NEP. Petro-Canada, a **crown corporation**, was formed to implement the NEP's policies. Once the Conservatives were elected to the federal government in 1984, the NEP was disbanded. Due hard feelings caused by the NEP, it was difficult for a Liberal, either federal or provincial, to become elected in Alberta.

1982

The Constitution Act

For years, Canada had been acting as a nation independent of British rule despite belonging to the British Empire. In matters of trade relations and international agreements, for example, Canada had been acting on its own behalf. Prime Minister Pierre Elliott Trudeau wanted to make Canada officially independent of Great Britain so that the country no longer need the

consent of its ruling country in matters affecting the nation. In 1982, Queen Elizabeth II and Prime Minister Trudeau signed the Canadian Constitution Act. The signing of the Constitution freed Canada from Great Britain's rule. Canada was now, officially, a sovereign country. The Constitution included a Charter of Rights and Freedoms. The charter guarantees certain political rights to Canadian citizens. It also ensures the civil rights of all residents of Canada. All provinces agreed to this act, except Quebec. The Quebec government wanted greater powers and recognition under the new Constitution. The Charlottetown and Meech Lake Accords were attempts at meeting the needs of the Quebec government in the hope of having the province sign the Constitution. However, both attempts failed.

1981

The federal government introduces the National Energy Program (NEP).

1982

The personal computer is introduced.

1983

The Western Grain Transportation Act is passed.

Canada U.S. Free Trade Agreement

1987

Canada–U.S. Free Trade Agreement

In 1987, Conservative Prime Minister Brian Mulroney and U.S. President Ronald Reagan met to discuss the creation of a free trade agreement between the two nations. This meeting became known as the Shamrock Summit because it was held on St. Patrick's Day and because both leaders were of Irish descent. This agreement helped establish a strong trading relationship between the two countries over the next decade. The agreement, which became known as the Canada-U.S. Free Trade Agreement (CUSFTA), eliminated tariffs, reduced non-tariff trade barriers, and was among the first trade agreements to include services as well as goods. CUSFTA was later replaced by the North American Free Trade Agreement (NAFTA.)

1984

Conservative leader Brian Mulroney becomes prime minister of Canada.

1985

The federal government eases laws that require companies to use the metric system.

Going Green

1986

The Canadian dollar is valued at 70.2 U.S. cents on international money markets. This is an all-time low.

1987

A stock market crash sparks the worst recession since the **Great Depression**.

Going Green

In the 1980s, the idea of "going green" became a mainstream idea. Environmental authorities kept a close eye on industry activities, alerting Canadians of any foul play when wilderness or wildlife was being affected. Protests to save Canada's old-growth forests from being logged by the forest industry made newspaper headlines. Environmental issues made the news again when the Inuit blamed Hydro-Quebec's massive James Bay power project for killing more than 20,000 caribou in 1984. The animals were swept away by rising river waters, caused by the opening of a dam upstream, and sent to their death when the swollen river carried them over a waterfall.

Cultural Exports, Eh!

Second City Television (SCTV) was a Canadian television show that made many Canadian comedians well-known around the world. The show first appeared on American airwaves in 1981. Comedians who appeared on the show included John Candy, Andrea Martin, Martin Short, Joe Flaherty, Eugene Levy, Dave Thomas, and Rick Moranis. Many of these Canadian comedians went on to have success on U.S. televisions shows, such as *Saturday Night Live*. Others starred in big-screen movies, many of which made millions of dollars. For example, Rick Moranis is well-known for his role in *Honey I Shrunk the Kids*, while Martin Short became a household name for his part in the Father of the Bride movies.

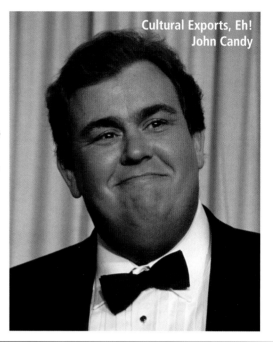

Cultural Exports, Eh!
John Candy

Into the Future

Computers have changed the way the world does business. Heralding in the Information Age, the personal computer was introduced in 1981. According to Beland Honderich, publisher of the *Toronto Star*, "Cheap, small and powerful computers are reaching into every sector of the economy... ." Personal computing was in its infancy in the 1980s, but it would be hard to imagine society without computers in the 21st century. How do you think computers will affect our lives in the future?

Calgary, Alberta, hosts the Winter Olympics, bringing millions of dollars in tourism revenue to the city.

The Canada-United States Free Trade Agreement (CUSFTA) comes into effect on January 1.

Fishery Products International closes three plants. About 1,300 people lose their jobs.

1970s

Stopping Pollution in the Great Lakes

1972

Stopping Pollution in the Great Lakes

In the 1960s, studies showed that the Great Lakes were highly polluted. Lakes Ontario and Erie were particularly affected. Canada blamed American industries for fouling the waters of the Great Lakes. The two nations recognized a need to resolve the issue. In 1972, the leaders of Canada and the United States, Prime Minister Trudeau and President Nixon respectively, signed an agreement called the Great Lakes Water Quality Act. This act was meant to help protect the water supply. The agreement is still in place today and has had several amendments over the years. The international community regards the act as a successful model of co-operation for restoring environmental quality and preventing future degradation.

1970

Canada becomes an official observer at OAS meetings.

1972

The James Bay Hydroelectric power project is started.

1973

Montreal holds Canada's first lottery to help fund the Summer Olympics.

1973

The Oil Crisis

Canada and other nations relied on oil to fuel their transportation needs, as well as machinery used to produce crops, plastics, and other products. Oil was available in high supply until 1973. The Organization of Arab Petroleum Exporting Countries (OAPEC), a group of Arab oil-producing countries, decided to limit oil exports, causing a spike in oil prices. By 1974, the price of oil had quadrupled. Across the eastern parts of Canada, the inflated oil rates were cause for crisis. Demand for oil from Alberta reached a high, earning the province a great deal of wealth. To help balance the crisis in the East with the economic boom in the West, the federal government formed a crown corporation called Petro-Canada. This new company was developed to help Canadians gain more control over its energy sector.

1974

Canada suspends exports of nuclear materials and equipment to India.

1975

To fight high inflation rates, Canada's federal government implements wage and price controls.

1976

The Birth of Petro-Canada

In 1973, the New **Democrat** Party introduced the bill for a publicly-owned oil and gas company. The concept came from the idea that oil reserves were being controlled by the U.S. market. Many countries had already established similar companies to gain control in the oil market. In 1975, the bill to create an oil and gas crown corporation was passed, and Petro-Canada was born. Petro-Canada received $1.5 billion in start up capital from the federal government and began operations in 1976. The head offices were located in Calgary, Alberta. In 2009, Petro-Canada and Suncor, a Canadian oil development and exploration company, announced plans for a merger. The move resulted in a combined revenue increase of $54.6 billion.

The Birth of Petro-Canada

1976

More than one million people hold a one-day strike in protest against wage and price controls.

1977

Canada's territorial waters are extended from a 19- to a 322-kilometre limit.

1978

VIA Rail is created.

1978

The G8

Canada joined the G8 in 1976. The G8 is a group of eight developed countries that have agreed to work with each other on issues such as national economies, international trade, relations with developing countries, terrorism, energy, and other concerns. Members of the G8 include Canada, France, Germany, Italy, Japan, Russia, Great Britain, and the United States. Top leaders from each of these nations attend G8 meetings to share their thoughts on matters of interest to all parties. G8 Summits are held every year and are hosted by member countries. Canada held its first G8 summit in 2002 in Kananaskis, Alberta.

The G8

Into the Future

The 1970s was a decade of economic independence for Canada. Wanting to reduce its reliance on the United States for trade, Canada began looking elsewhere to sell its goods. In 1970, Canada formally recognized the Communist Party of China as the official government of China. Goods made in China fuelled the big box, or department, stores that later came on stream in the 1980s. Can you think of any items you own that have been made in China?

1979

U.S.-controlled Pacific Petroleums is purchased by Petro-Canada.

1980

The National Energy Program (NEP) is introduced.

Trade and Global Impact
1960s

Trudeaumania
Pierre Elliott Trudeau

1960s

Trudeaumania

In early 1968, Pierre Elliott Trudeau was the Liberal candidate running for prime minister. He was a charismatic speaker with new ideas. Across the country, particularly among young Canadians, there was a great deal of excitement surrounding Trudeau. This wave of excitement was called "Trudeaumania." Trudeau was elected prime minister of Canada in 1968. After being elected to office, excitement surrounding Trudeau continued. This interest in Trudeau inspired a board game released in the 1980s, called "True Dough Mania."

1961

Canadian University Service Overseas (CUSO) is formed to provide aid to Third World countries.

1962

The Trans-Canada Highway officially opens.

1963

Lester B. Pearson becomes prime minister of Canada.

Trans-Canada Highway Route

Yukon
Territory

Northwest Territories

Nunavut
Territories

British
Columbia

Newfoundland
and Labrador

Alberta

Saskatchewan

Manitoba

Québec

Prince Edward
Island

Ontario

Nova Scotia

New
Brunswick

Trans-canada Highway
ROUTE

CANADA

300   0   300   600   900
km   km

1962

Trans-Canada Highway

The Trans-Canada Highway was built to serve Canada's growing population. It was to provide a fast and efficient transportation route for the country's people and goods. Starting in St. John's, Newfoundland, this massive road project, spreading across the entire country, ended in Victoria, British Columbia. The highway officially opened in 1962, with the completion of the Rogers Pass section through the Rockies in British Columbia. One of the longest roads in the world, the Trans-Canada Highway's reach is 7,821 km (4,860 miles). A white maple leaf on a green background is the symbol of the Trans-Canada Highway. The symbol can be seen on road signs across the nation.

Trans-Canada Highway

1964

Canadians receive social insurance cards for the first time.

1965

Canada and the United States sign the Auto Pact.

Auto Pact

Canada's small auto industry was not doing much to bolster Canada's sagging economy in the early 1960s. Prior to 1965, Canada had a trade deficit when it came to cars. The country **imported** far more cars from the United States than it exported. Canada wanted to sell more cars into the large U.S. market, and the United States wanted Canada to reduce its 17 percent auto import tax so it could sell more U.S.-made cars in Canada. In 1965, the two nations' auto industries merged with the signing of the Canada-United States Automotive Products Agreement, called the Auto Pact. Tariffs were removed, making it affordable for both Canada and the United States to expand their car-making operations. The Auto Pact meant a single North American automobile market had been established. The Auto Pact was a limited free trade agreement as it included built-in safeguards for Canada. For example, all cars built in Canada had to have 60 percent Canadian parts and labour, and Canada had to build one car for every U.S.-built car sold in Canada.

Auto Pact

1966
The Canada Pension Plan begins.

1967
Canada celebrates its 100th year as a nation by hosting Expo 67.

1968
Canada's army, navy, and air force are united as one entity.

Expo 67
================

Expo 67

Canada invited the world to Expo 67, a world fair taking place the year of Canada's 100th birthday. A World Fair is a large public exhibition that takes place in a different part of the world each year. Expo 67 was a six-month-long event that took place in Montreal, Quebec. Themed "Man and His World," almost 120 governments were represented at the event, which included six 'theme' pavilions, 48 national pavilions, four provincial pavilions, 27 private-industry and institutional pavilions. In addition, thousands of private exhibitors and sponsors participated in 53 private pavilions and facilities. People came from across the country and all over the world to take part in Expo 67. The increase in tourist revenues directly related to Expo 67 amounted to $480 million. This was much more than the $283 million cost to build and run the fair.

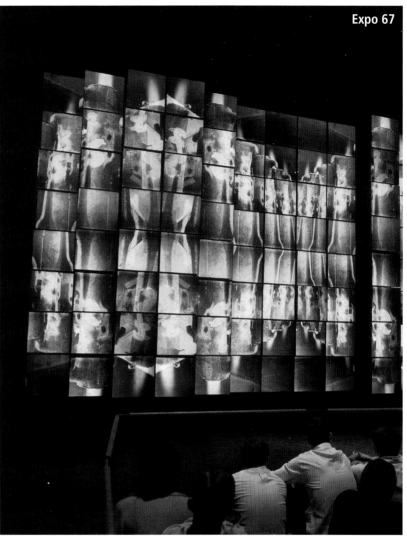

Canada was once again selected to host the World's Fair in 1986. Vancouver, British Columbia, was the host city.

Into the Future

Expo 67 helped Canada showcase its best features to countries around the world. One of Canada's most prominent features is the fact that it is home to people whose heritage spans the world, from Europe and Asia to Africa, Australia, and the Americas. Canada is a multicultural country. What are some of the benefits that come from living in a multicultural country?

1969

Canada signs a treaty discouraging the development of nuclear weapons.

1970

The Hudson's Bay Company headquarters move to Winnipeg, Manitoba.

Transportation

Boom Time!

1951

Boom Time!

The 1950s was a time of prosperity for many Canadians. The generation born during this era would become known as the "baby boomers." This group was called the baby boomers because of the increased number of babies that were born after soldiers returned from World War II. The baby boomers became a powerful consumer demographic for many decades. Many companies developed products just to cater to this demographic. The baby boom resulted in a need to develop suburban communities to house the increase in families looking to buy houses. Strip malls and shopping centres were then

1950s

Transportation

Transportation routes were needed for the efficient shipping of trade goods across the country. In the 1950s, massive transportation construction projects took place on land, water, and even underground. The Trans-Canada Highway, which began construction in 1950, the St. Lawrence Seaway, and the Toronto subway were three major transportation projects undertaken or completed in the 1950s. The Toronto subway was Canada's first completed subway. This subway includes 69 stations and is 70 kilometres long. The St. Lawrence Seaway is a system of canals, locks, and channels that allows ships to travel from the Atlantic Ocean to the Great Lakes. Construction of the seaway was approved in 1954, and it was completed in 1959.

1951

The St. Lawrence Seaway Authority is created.

1952

Canada spends $2 billion, or two-fifths of its federal budget, on defence.

built to serve the shopping needs of the baby boomers. With the new appealing destinations came the need for transportation. The boom caused automobile manufacturing to rise dramatically, as people needed cars to transport their families. In 1956, Canadians bought 400,000 automobiles. By the end of the decade, Canadians had purchased more than 3.5 million new cars.

1954

The Cold War

The Cold War was a time of continual political, military, and economic upset. Tensions between the United States and the Soviet Union resulted in the threat of a nuclear attack from another country. Canada, located between the Soviet Union and the United States of America, was at risk for a Soviet air strike. The United States saw Canada's North as critical for defending against a nuclear attack. A line of radar stations, called the Distant Early Warning (DEW) Line, were set up in the Canadian North, as well as in Alaska and Greenland, to detect any unauthorized Soviet aircrafts. Fighter planes were also on standby in North Bay, Ontario, to intercept potential Soviet bombers. The Cold War is considered to have come to an end in 1989 with the fall of the Berlin Wall.

The Cold War

1953

Elizabeth II is crowned queen of Great Britain.

1954

The Toronto subway opens. It is Canada's first underground transit system.

1955

The Toronto-Dominion Bank is formed.

1957

Canada Council

Canada's culture is exported when a painting is put on display, a theatre company or dance group tours another country, a book written by a Canadian author is sold in another country, or a Canadian television show is sold to an international network. In 1957, the federal government created the Canada Council for the Arts to help promote the study and enjoyment of the arts. The Canada Council is a crown corporation that distributes grants, endowments, and prizes to Canadian artists. Artists working in the areas of visual arts, dance, theatre, writing, music, and performing arts can apply to the Canada Council for funding support. The Canada Council's financial support of Canadian artists has helped the country build a cultural industry worth millions of dollars in revenues.

Canada Council

1956

A law that guarantees equal pay for women is passed by the Canadian government.

1957

The Canada Council is established to encourage the development of the arts and social sciences in Canada.

1959

Eight Poets

In 1959, the Canada Council gave eight poets $25 each, plus travel expenses, to give poetry readings. This initiative was done to promote Canadian artists. Leonard Cohen, who became one of Canada's foremost poets and singer-songwriters, was one of the artists to receive the grant. Cohen's first book of poetry was published in 1956. Seven years later, he published his first novel. In the 1960s, Cohen began recording music. He is known around the world for his songwriting, and more than 2,000 versions of his songs, including the well-known *Hallelujah*, have been recorded by various artists. Cohen has been inducted in the Canadian Music Hall of Fame, the Canadian Songwriters Hall of Fame, and American Rock and Roll Hall of Fame.

Eight Poets
Leonard Cohen

Into the Future

In the post-war decade of the 1950s, Canada was beginning to shape its own identity, separate from that of Great Britain. From the creation of the Canada Council to earning a certain level of self-governance, Canada showcased its independence to the world. What do you think makes Canadian culture unique?

1958

The Royal Commission on Canada's Economic Prospects suggests laws to keep ownership of banks and financial companies within Canada.

1959

The St. Lawrence Seaway opens.

1960

The National Gallery opens in Ottawa.

Military Dependence

1941	1942	1943
Canada and United States sign the Ogdensburg Agreement on Hemispheric Defence.	The Canadian government holds a national vote on conscription.	Canada gives Great Britain weapons of war worth $1 billion.

Military Dependence

In the early years of World War II, the European continent was controlled by Nazi Germany. If Great Britain fell to Nazi Germany, Canada feared that it would become Germany's next target. Both Canada and the United States were concerned about their defence vulnerabilities. As a result, President Franklin Delano Roosevelt shared his plan with Prime Minister William Lyon Mackenzie King to form a joint board to supervise the defence of both Canada and the United States throughout World War II and in the future. The two countries signed the Ogdensburg Agreement in August 1940. The agreement developed economic and military planning through the Permanent Joint Board on Defence. This was the start of Canada's military reliance on the United States.

1940s

Canada Supports World War II

About 60 percent of Canada's production was for war use between 1939 and 1945. In addition to sending about 1.1 million troops overseas to fight in World War II, Canada supported the war effort by producing 28,000 pieces of heavy **artillery**, 1.5 million rifles and machine guns, 100 million rounds of heavy-calibre artillery ammunition, 4.4 billion rounds of small-calibre ammunition, 800,000 military vehicles, and 6,500 tanks. Canada produced 16,200 airplanes of all types and 8,000 ships.

Canada Supports World War II

1944

British Columbia budgets $6 million to link Prince George, British Columbia, with the Alaska Highway in the United States.

1945

The World Bank is formed by the United Nations.

31

Victory War Bonds

In 1946, the government of Canada created a concept meant to help Canadians reach their savings and investment goals. People were offered the opportunity to purchase Victory War Bonds. A bond is a government certificate that promises repayment of borrowed funds by a certain date and at a fixed rate of interest. The Victory War Bonds were introduced as part of the country's postwar financial plan and offered people a safe way to invest their money. The bonds guaranteed minimum amount of interest on any money used to purchase them. By 1946, people could purchase bonds through their work payroll. At the time, about 16,000 employers participated in the program. Victory War Bonds eventually became known as Canada Savings Bonds. Today, many people purchase the bonds as part of their savings plan. The bonds are offered for sale each year between the months of October and April.

Victory War Bonds

1946

Canada earns its own seat at the United Nations.

1947

The General Agreement on Tariffs and Trade (GATT) is established.

1948

A three percent sales tax is introduced in British Columbia to help pay for social programs.

1948

GATT

The General Agreement on Tariffs and Trade (GATT) came into effect on January 1, 1948. This agreement was developed to provide a forum to promote free trade between its members. It would do this by reducing and regulating tariffs on traded goods. This agreement also provided a means for resolving trade disputes. Twenty-three countries, including Canada, signed the GATT in 1947. GATT became the basis for all trade relations between Canada and the United States. The Most Favoured Nation (MFN) rule of GATT stated that any member country must give all other members the same trading

NATO

privileges that it would give to its most favoured trade partner. Today, more than 110 countries are members of GATT.

1949

NATO

Canada's participation in the North Atlantic Treaty Organization (NATO) represented the country's first peacetime military alliance. NATO, a concept that involved a collective military defence, was the idea of the Canadian Department of External Affairs.

All NATO members agreed to defend each other should one nation be attacked by a non-member nation. During the Cold War, NATO members were concerned about defending themselves and each other from an attack, especially a nuclear attack by the Soviet Union. The treaty to form NATO was signed in 1949 by Canada, the United States, and 10 western European countries. Its first leader, Lord Ismay, said NATO's role was, "to keep the Russians out, the Americans in, and the Germans down."

GATT

Into the Future

The first half of the 1940s was war-torn. Families were divided as husbands and fathers travelled overseas to fight. While the men were away, women went to work in factories to make bombs and other weapons of war, and to help keep essential services running. How do you feel these women influenced women's rights today?

1949

Canada joins the North Atlantic Treaty Organization (NATO).

1950

Canada fights in the Korean War as part of the United Nations force.

Canada's Voice is Heard
William Lyon Mackenzie King

1931
Canada gains independence from Great Britain.

1932
Canada hosts the first Imperial Economic Conference ever held outside London, England.

1933
The Great Depression reaches its peak in Canada.

1931

Canada's Voice is Heard

The Statute of Westminster came into effect on December 11, 1931. It gave legislative equality to self-governing dominions of the British Empire. Prior to the creation of this statute, Great Britain continued to hold certain powers over its dominions, as well as overriding authority. The statute was signed by Canadian Prime Minister William Lyon Mackenzie King, and Canada was given control over its foreign affairs. This included matters of trade as well as the right to declare war. No longer would Canada's voice be heard only through its mother country. In effect, the Statute of Westminster gave Canada and other dominions of Great Britian independence. Less than a year after the statute was signed, Canada hosted the first Imperial Economic Conference outside of London, England. The conference, which focussed on the Great Depression, included colonies and dominions of Great Britain.

1933

The Great Depression

The Great Depression reached its peak in Canada in 1933, with about 20 per cent of Canadians receiving some form of government relief. Canada relied on trading its natural resources of lumber and minerals, as well as its manufactured goods, with the United States. When the United States' demand for Canadian goods decreased, Canadian economics suffered. With export earnings down, thousands of workers were laid off from their jobs. By 1933, 27 per cent of Canada's labour force was unemployed. Prairie farmers were affected, too. A drought of several years turned their once-fertile land into nothing more than a dust bowl, making it impossible to grow crops. Two-thirds of Saskatchewan's population was on government relief, and the province's income dropped by 90 percent.

The Great Depression

1934

The Bank of Canada is created.

1935

The Bank of Canada opens its doors. On March 11, 1935, the Bank of Canada issues its first series of bank notes.

Trans-Canada Airlines

Trans-Canada Airlines (TCA) first took flight in 1937. Canada's newly formed Department of Transport wanted an airline that could service all of Canada. The airline was created through legislation from the federal government. It was a subsidiary company of Canadian National Railways (CNR), a crown corporation, and was given $5 million in start up funding from the government. The airline grew from a small company with two-passenger planes used for surveying to a major passenger and cargo airline. In its early days, TCA competed directly for passengers with its parent railway company. As airline passenger service grew, with new routes across the country and overseas, railway passenger service declined. By 1964, TCA had become Canada's national airline. A year later, its name was changed to Air Canada.

Trans-Canada Airlines

1936

The Vimy Ridge Memorial, designed by Walter Seymour Allward, is unveiled in France.

1937

Trans-Canada Airlines is created.

World War II

The start of World War II helped bring the world out of economic depression at the end of the decade. This global military conflict started on September 1, 1939, when anti-democratic Nazi Germany invaded Poland. Canada fought on the side of the **Allies** to put a stop to Germany's leader, Adolf Hitler, and the Nazi regime. More than 100 million military personnel were involved in World War II, and about 70 million people died as a result of this war. Most of them were civilians. After the fall of Germany, the United States and the Soviet Union emerged as the world's two superpowers, setting the stage for the Cold War.

World War II
Joseph Goebbels (left)
and Adolf Hitler

Into the Future

The Great Depression was a time of hardship for millions of people across North America. Being jobless, homeless, and hungry was a common situation for many people. The coming of war, despite the devastation, brought prosperity. Unemployed men became employed once they joined the military. Men and women worked in factories to build weapons and vehicles. Can you think of any other ways that the war may have impacted the economy?

1938
Franklin Delano Roosevelt becomes the first U.S. president to visit Canada.

1939
Canada establishes High Commissions in Ireland, New Zealand, Australia, and South Africa.

1940
Canada and the United States sign the Ogdensburg Agreement on Hemispheric Defence.

A Decade of Prosperity

1921

The Canadian Authors Association (CAA) is formed to promote writers and their works.

1922

For the first time ever, U.S. investment in Canada is greater than that of Great Britain.

A Decade of Prosperity

The early 1920s was a time of prosperity in North America. Large-scale wheat production on the Prairies contributed to Canada exporting enough wheat to provide more than half of the world's supply. Canada's growing pulp and paper industry exported newsprint around the world. Investors looking for a fast and easy way to earn money, invested in finding and mining Canada's metals and minerals. These metals and minerals were then exported to clients in other countries. Transportation and telecommunications also expanded with new railroad tracks and cars, deepened harbours, and improved telephone services. Hydroelectric dams were built to meet the increased demand for electricity. There was no sign of economic slowdown in Canada until the crash of the New York Stock Exchange late in the decade.

United States Investment in Canada

Canada and the United States first signed a free trade agreement in 1854. Twelve years later, it was terminated by the United States. Though Canada sent more than 50 percent of its exports to Great Britain and only 40 percent to the United States, it wanted to open the doors to its southern neighbour once again. This was primarily because about 60 percent of Canada's imports came from the United States. In 1911, Canada and the United States announced a **reciprocal** trade agreement that removed and reduced tariffs on a number of goods being traded across the border. Americans began investing heavily in Canada. By 1922, U.S. investment in Canada was greater than that of Great Britain.

United States Investment in Canada

1923

The Halibut Fisheries Treaty is signed between Canada and the United States.

1924

The Royal Canadian Air Force is established on April 1.

1925

Chrysler Canada opens a plant in Windsor, Ontario.

39

Fish and Canadian Independence

1923

Fish and Canadian Independence

An agreement between Canada and the United States on fishing rights marked the beginning of Canada's independence from Great Britain. In 1923, the Halibut Treaty was signed between Canada and the United States, without Great Britain's involvement or approval. The government of Great Britain wanted to sign the agreement, but Canadian Prime Minister William Lyon Mackenzie King rejected the idea. He believed Great Britain should not negotiate on Canada's behalf. This treaty was developed to protect significantly depleted halibut stocks by closing the fishing season for three months each year.

1929

Stock Market Crash

On October 29, 1929, the New York stock exchange crashed. This resulted in a global economic downturn lasting about 10 years. Many people lost their all of their money because of the crash. This, in turn, bankrupted both banks and businesses. Many jobs were lost, which resulted in hardship for individuals and families. Without a paycheque, there was no money to pay for food and lodging. People were left homeless and hungry. Canada's export market was destroyed, also contributing to massive job losses. Other countries placed protective tariffs on many goods during this time. Protective tariffs are used to inflate the prices of products that are imported from other countries. Inflated import prices help promote the sale of products made by domestic industries because they are more reasonably priced. The decision to use protective tariffs resulted in a collapse in world trade.

1926

Great Britain agrees that its dominions, including Canada, should be self-governing.

1927

The Old Age Pensions Act is introduced.

Into the Future

The stock market crash caused the worldwide economy to crumble. What circumstances led to the stock market crash? The world experienced a similar economic "bust" in the 2000s. How was this situation similar or different from the one in the 1920s? What can be done to help ensure the world does not experience another economic downturn like the one faced in recent years?

1928

Pier 21 in Halifax greets and assesses immigrants to Canada.

1929

The New York Stock Exchange crashes.

1930

The Conservative Party wins a majority in the federal election.

The Treaty of Versailles

1914

Progress Paces Ahead

Canada had the world's fastest-growing economy between 1896 and the start of World War I in 1914. This was due, in large part, to the many important technological advances were taking place in this period. Innovations, such as automobiles, radio, telephone, and the electric light, were being invented by people in all parts of the world. Each of these inventions contributed to Canada's progress by helping make daily activities, cross-country travel, and business communications more efficient.

1919

The Treaty of Versailles

The Treaty of Versailles was one of the peace treaties that ended World War I. When it came time to sign the Treaty of Versailles in 1919, Canada felt it had earned the right to do so independently of Great Britain. Canada supported World War I in many ways, including providing men to serve as soldiers. Canadian farms fed troops overseas, and Canadian factories produced goods, from ammunition to uniforms, for the troops to use in battle. Signing the treaty marked the beginning of Canada's independence in foreign policy.

1911	1914	1915
Robert Borden becomes prime minister of Canada.	Oil is discovered in Turner Valley.	Construction of the Canadian Northern Railway line to Vancouver is completed.

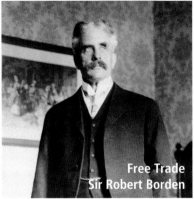

Free Trade
Sir Robert Borden

World War I

1911

Free Trade

Free trade between Canada and the United States has been a long-standing issue for both nations. A reciprocity agreement between the two countries was the main issue of the September 1911 federal election in Canada. This agreement was promoted by Liberal Prime Minister Wilfred Laurier. However, many Canadians did not see the need for free trade, as the country was experiencing a period of great prosperity at the time. Opponents to the idea of free trade were also concerned it could allow a takeover of

Canada by the United States. Laurier lost the election to Conservative leader Robert Borden. The Conservatives were against free trade until the 1980s, when Prime Minister Brian Mulroney ushered in a new free trade agreement between Canada and the United States.

1916

World War I

World War I began in August 1914, when Great Britain declared war on Germany. Canada chose to fight in the war and did so under British military command. Canadians were commended for their efforts during battles, such as Vimy Ridge, in which they were able to conquer enemy lines where other Allied forces had previously failed. Due to their successes at war, many Canadians started thinking of themselves as Canadians first and British subjects second. They began to consider seeking independence from Great Britain and self-governance.

1918

On the Home Front

In 1918, women gained the right to vote in Canada's federal elections, giving them a say in how the country was governed. Women also worked in factories to offset the shortage of labourers caused by men going overseas participate in the war. Canada's production of goods increased between 1910 and 1918. The gross value of the production of textiles, iron and steel, and transportation equipment increased about 300 percent each.

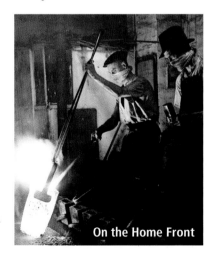

On the Home Front

1916

The National Transcontinental Railway (NTR), running from Moncton to Winnipeg, is completed.

1920

Great Britain declares war on Germany, and World War I begins.

Trade and Global Impact
1900s

Automotive Production Begins in Canada

Natural Resources Build Economy

Big Projects, Big Dreams

1900s

Automotive Production Begins in Canada

In the late 1800s, U.S. inventor Henry Ford developed the first horseless carriage. By 1903, he had incorporated the Ford Motor Company. Within one year, Ford had signed a deal with Canadian businessman Gordon M. McGregor to bring automobile manufacturing to Canada. McGregor's company earned the right to assemble Ford cars for all countries in the British Empire, with the exception of Great Britain.

1900s

Natural Resources Build Economy

Canada was heavily dependent on the extraction and export of its natural resources to fuel its economy. Timber from Canada's vast forests was traded so other countries could build ships and construct buildings. **Klondike** gold and other minerals, such as copper and silver, were also in demand around the world. In the 1900s, most of Canada's international trade was with Great Britain. Great Britain gave Canada and its other colonies preferential trade. When a country is considered a preferential trading area (PTA), tariffs are reduced to allow for easier import of products from that country. Canada could now export products to Great Britain with fewer limitations.

1900s

Big Projects, Big Dreams

The 1900s saw a dramatic increase in large construction projects from coast to coast. This activity was in response to a growing population and an expanding economy. From bridge building to railway construction, many projects were undertaken by governments to move people and goods more efficiently. Other projects, such as the construction of factories, were completed by private companies. The prospect of a finding a job working on construction projects made the dream of prosperity in Canada a

1904

Henry Ford opens a plant in Canada on August 17.

1906

The Revillion Freres trading post opens in Fort Saint John as competition to the Hudson's Bay Company.

Canada Strengthens U.S. Ties

reality. Investors from both Great Britain and the United States helped fuel Canada's economic growth by investing in many of the projects.

1903

Alaska Boundary Dispute

For years, Canada and the United States had been locked in a dispute over the Alaska boundary. When the United States purchased Alaska from Russia, it gained control of areas that Canada felt should belong to it instead. In 1903, the two countries agreed to appoint an Alaskan Boundary Tribunal to resolve the dispute. The tribunal included a panel of six judges, three from the United States, two from Canada, and one from Great Britain. Canada had hoped that the British would support Canadian interests. However, Great Britain needed the United States' assistance in an arms race with Germany. After three weeks of discussion, the panel of judges voted in favour the United States' position.

1909

Canada Strengthens U.S. Ties

In response to the 1903 Alaska boundary dispute, Canada formed its own Department of External Affairs in 1909. Canada could now better look after its own foreign affairs, such as trade negotiations and setting boundaries, instead of relying on Great Britain to look after Canadian interests. In 1909, Canada also wanted to strengthen its ties to the United States. This was accomplished by setting up the International Joint Commission to investigate and find solutions to potential disputes between Canada and the United States.

Alaska Boundary Dispute

1907

Anti-Japanese riots take place. Both Canadian and Japanese governments agree to limit Japanese immigration.

1908

The Royal Canadian Mint is founded in Ottawa.

1909

The International Joint Commission is formed.

ACTIVITY
Into the Future

The essence of trade is exchanging a good or service for another good or service in return. To do this, people negotiate to strike a balance that, ideally, works for all parties. All successful deals have one thing in common, the successful art of negotiation.

Every day, people around the world negotiate the prices of good and services, such as automobiles and haircuts. Some cultures are more open to negotiating. For example, in North America, it is common to negotiate the price of a car at an auto dealer. Yet, in other countries, the car will be sold for no less than what is posted on the ticket. Negotiation can be used for more than determining the price of goods and services. It is also used in other aspects of life. For example, a child might negotiate a later bedtime for a Friday night or special occasion.

Become a Negotiator

Think about a good or service that you would like to buy or receive. Determine who it is that can give you this good or service. This person might be a parent, a teacher, an employer, or a friend. What can you offer in return for this good or service? You may offer time, labour, money, or a trade. Develop a strategy to convince the person you are trading with to give you the good or service. Think about ways to overcome possible objections to your trade offer. Negotiate a proposition where both sides of the trade feel as if they have benefited from the exchange. Assess the results. Did you get what you wanted at a "price" you could afford? Did the other person get what he or she wanted or needed in exchange? Did both parties feel fairly treated at the end of the negotiation?

FURTHER
Research

Many books and websites provide information on Canada's foreign affairs of trade and global impact. To learn more about these topics, borrow books from the library or surf the Internet.

Books

Most libraries have computers that connect to a database of books for researching information. By entering a "key word" you will be provided with a list of books in the library that contain information on that topic. Non-fiction books are arranged numerically, according to their call number. Fiction books are organized alphabetically by the author's last name.

Websites

For information on Canada's foreign affairs, including trade and global impact, visit the Government of Canada's website at **www.international.gc.ca**

For more information on the Genuine Progress Indicator (GPI), visit **www.greeneconomics.ca/gpi**

Glossary

Allies: the nations that joined to fight against Germany and its associates during World Wars I and II, including Great Britain, France, Canada, the United States, and Russia

artillery: large guns, such as cannons, mortars, and missile launchers

carbon emissions: harmful substances discharged into the air, such as car exhaust

crown corporation: a commercial company owned by the Canadian government that is managed independently from the government

democrat: a person who supports a system of government that is elected by the entire population of a certain place

economy: the production and consumption of goods and services by a group, such as a community or a country

exports: outgoing goods sold by one country to another

free trade: international trade without restrictions or tariffs

Great Depression: a period of global economic slowdown that followed the New York Stock Exchange crash of 1929; characterized by high prices for goods, unemployment, and poverty

Gross Domestic Product (GDP): the total value of goods and services produced by a nation in a year, less net income from investments in other countries

imported: brought in goods from another country

Information Age: a time when people can communicate with one another or gain instant access to information through computers and the Internet

Klondike: an area in the Yukon where large amounts of gold were found

labour mobility: the ability of workers to cross borders and carry on work in their chosen profession without first being approved or re-certified

mortgage pools: a group of mortgages that have similar maturity dates and interest rates and are used to secure another asset

petro dollar: the value of a dollar based on oil instead of gold

reciprocal: a relationship involving the mutual exchange of goods and services

trade deficit: when the value of imports is greater than the value of exports

Index